TRINANT
IN PHOTOGRAPHS
with
ABERBEEG, LLANHILLETH, CRUMLIN, KENDON and OAKDALE

Volume 1

by Clive Daniels

Foreword by
TREVOR WILDE

Old Bakehouse Publications

Abertillery

First published in November 1995

ISBN 1 874538 80 8

Published in the U.K. by
Old Bakehouse Publications
Church Street,
Abertillery, Gwent NP3 1EA
Telephone: 01495 212600   Fax: 01495 216222

Made and printed in the UK
by J.R. Davies (Printers) Ltd.

Foreword
by Trevor Wilde

I consider it a great honour to be associated with this volume, there being a nostalgia in all such editions, that awakens the memory and old friends are remembered and those so sweet occasions are, for a moment, re-lived.

Therefore, my first duty is to thank the author for his ingenuity and skill in compiling this volume. Well done Clive.

Trinant of the 30s was comprised of Pentwyn Inn, the fourteen houses, The Rank and Wesley Terrace, with a few houses dotted round about. But its inhabitants lacked nothing in their social vitality. Councillor Sidney Holloway, Ernie Daniels and Freddie Smith ran the ambulance class in the village. Olwen Davies ran its youth club.

The Wesleyan Chapel was a hive of activity, as was Horeb Chapel, perched there on the brow of the hill as we leave Trinant. It was at the anniversary service in Horeb, that I did my first public engagement, in 1932.

A visit to Llwyncellyn Farm on Sunday afternoons, would find Llew Williams rehearsing the male voice choir, in the lounge.

These many activities bonded the community of Trinant into the like activities of the surrounding valleys. It was considered a nice evening out to meander up to Pentwyn by the people of Aberbeeg, Llanhilleth, Brynithel and Oakdale, that pretty little mining village lying just to the west.

Remembering that the womenfolk had to walk for their weekly shopping, Crumlin and Llanhilleth demanded regular visits.

The church and chapel life was so intense that inter-visits were frequent with the people of Brynithel, Llanhilleth, Oakdale and Aberbeeg.

The Workingmen's Hall at Llanhilleth was at one time a hive of activity, as was the Community Hall at Oakdale. The closure of the mines, where the men-folk of all these communities interwove their working lives has now ceased and might have halted the daily encounter, but the bond created during that era will remain for many years.

I hope this volume will rekindle some of those lovely memories in the minds of the people of these communities and help those memories to live for a long time in the minds of their children.

Trevor Wilde

Contents

Introduction

Having lived my entire 64 years in the village of Trinant, which means 'Three Brooks', it is only in recent times have I really started to reminisce and ask myself a question or two about the locale. Where had all those years disappeared to and what had happened I wondered, to the many friends and faces who had once occupied this mountainside village? My thoughts then turned to considering documentation of some of my memories and those of fellow citizens, in an attempt at recording them for posterity. As with so many South Wales towns and villages, the appearance has changed beyond recognition in recent years, aided by the decease of a once flourishing coal industry which gave not only prosperity, but a certain amount of heartache too. The accompanying trades of Iron and Steel manufacture and a railway system which once contributed to the bustling noise of a valley in motion have all gone too, to say nothing of the changes in social attitudes which have forced the closure and demolition of so many of our places of worship and other long established buildings.

The purpose of this book is to try and record some of our local history and its people through the media of the interminable photograph combined with the memories of the many local people to whom I have spoken. There are many familiar faces and personalities of a kind to be seen within these pages, together with numerous views of the district which I hope will invoke a few memories, particularly of those former inhabitants who have sought pastures new but somehow, have acquired a copy of this book.

To concentrate solely on Trinant would not of course have been considerate or practical, I have therefore extended the work to include the neighbourhoods of Aberbeeg, Llanhilleth, Crumlin, Kendon and Oakdale. Again, the populace of these hamlets will I hope, derive much pleasure in scanning through the pages reviving some far-flung memories. Many will remember, while others should be aware of once towering Crumlin Viaduct and the 19th century skills which created it. Many residents of Oakdale will recall its record breaking colliery and the eminent Workmens Institute, once the centre of village social life, now resting in restored condition at The Museum of Welsh Life at St Fagans, Cardiff. The spirits of Llanhilleth and Aberbeeg with their peoples are also represented with a selection of photographs which show a number of generations.

I am truly indebted to the many folk of the district who have loaned photographs and given so freely of their time in helping me compile this book. I also wish to thank, well known local elocutionist Mr Trevor Wilde who kindly agreed to write the foreword. I would also like to extend my sincere thanks to fellow author of several local books Mr Malcolm Thomas for his help and encouragement in producing this volume.

Clive Daniels

CHAPTER 1
In and Around Trinant

1. To commence the book, here is a superb aerial view of Trinant and Cwmnant photographed in 1993.

2. This is an alternative view of the district, that of The Pant, Trinant.

PT.3. ABERBEEG VALLEY. PENTWYN TRINANT.

3./4. Two views, both taken from Pentwyn, Trinant of the Aberbeeg and Glandwr valley. These scenes probably date from the mid 1960s.

PT.4. ABERBEEG VALLEY. PENTWYN TRINANT.

5. Long Row Trinant c.1930. This was a row of twelve houses known as 'The Rank', built in the mid 19th century in typical Welsh cottage design. By today's standards they provided meagre accommodation with ten of the houses having one bedroom upstairs and one room down. The fortunate occupants of just two, had the luxury of two bedrooms and one room down. There were no rear entrances, no bathrooms, coal was stored inside and the toilets were outside a few yards away! The Rank was demolished in 1939 and the residents rehoused at Pentwyn Terrace.

6. Above are some of the children who lived in The Rank in the 1920s and 1930s. Left to right, back row: Kenneth Morrisey, Doreen Weybourne, Iris Morgan. Second row: Dennis Holyfield, Hilda Morgan, Ceinwen Richards, Betty Rowley, Pamela Rowley, Desmond Richards. Third row: Brian Holyfield, Mary Rowley, Clifford Morgan. Front row: Clive Holyfield, Brenda Holyfield, Thelma Morrisey, Jean Addis, Muriel Morgan, Raymond Richards.

7./8. Both of these bungalows were built around 1920 from army huts used in the First World War. The bungalow above, known as Bridge View, was built for the Skuse family, and the one below for the Watts family. They were lived in until the early 1980s.

9.   Pictured from Pentwyn Trinant, is this 1960s look at Cwmnant and Pentrepiod.

10.   Probably taken the same time as the photograph at the top of the page is this view of The Pant and Pentwyn.

11./12. Above, is Pant Square, Trinant as it appeared in the year 1930. Looking carefully, one can see a unique old oil street lamp which once stood in the centre of the square. Below, is the same scene, some 65 years later and this well illustrates the numerous changes that have taken place, particulary, extensive housing development.

13./14. Two differing views of Pentrepiod, with some 50 years separating them. Above is the scene as pictured through the eyes of Mattie Kibby from her painting of 1940. Below is a photograph taken at the same spot in 1995, showing how modern bungalows have replaced the old cottages and the extension of the original lane to make way for a new roadway to link up with the Pen-y-Fan Industrial Estate.

15. Pen-y-Fan Pond was planned and constructed during the very early years of the 19th century to supply water to the Crumlin arm of the Monmouthshire canal. Before reaching the canal itself, water was channelled overland to Croespenmaen where it was used to drive the Tony-y-Felin Mill. From there it was piped down the Kendon Hill to Crumlin, feeding the canal at a point in front of the Viaduct Hotel. This was the site of a warehouse where goods and materials were stored ready for transport along the waterway. These days Pen-y-Fan Pond serves as a tourist attraction and has been developed as such by the Gwent County Council and Islwyn Borough Council with financial assistance from the Countryside Commission. The pond has a capacity of 40 million gallons of water with depths of up to 17 feet, covering an area of 17½ acres, the size of 11 rugby pitches. Pen-y-Fan Country Park was opened on 23rd May 1976 by Mr John S Cripps CBE, chairman of the Countryside Commission. Various water and sailing activities are permitted and the site attracts more than 80,000 visitors per year, it is also the venue for the annual Country Fair held in June.

16. This is a picture of the Pant Trinant in 1947. To the right of the school can be seen Yew Tree Cottages whilst above are Llanerch Cottages.

17. This is Pentwyn Road, a typical 1950's street scene with just one motor car and one cyclist occupying the roadway. As to be seen in this view, at the top of the street was an attractive avenue of horse chestnut trees, and dry stone walls leading to the farm's outer buildings which have now unfortunately disappeared in the wake of progress.

C. DAVIES

TRINANT SERVICE STATION

TRINANT Nr. CRUMLIN MON.

National Benzole Petrols

Repairs, Tyres and Accessories

18. Mr John Tucker outside his shop in Trinant. He became the first Postmaster when he opened the Post Office in his General Stores in the late 1920s. It would be impossible to recognise the precise whereabouts of this original Post Office today, but some clues are, the building was later to become the Workmen's Club and these days it is the decorative private dwelling known as 'Greenfield House'.

19. Mr. George Handy standing in the doorway of his General Store at Church Street, Abertillery in around 1906. Mr Handy moved to Trinant and opened a shop there named 'Handy's Stores', that shop is now the premises of Trinant's Post Office.

20. A timeworn stone stile which was erected at Lower Cefn Coch Farm by its then owner Edmund Howell in the year 1851.

21. A century later and haymaking is in progress at Cefn Coch. Among the farm workers and holding the horse's reins is Mr Ted Jones.

22.   A rural scene at the cottages, Cefn Coch in 1948. The children to be seen here are Jimmy Lucas, Veronica Lucas, Molly Bessant and Marjorie Lucas.

23.   To illustrate progress and what a difference 47 years can make, here is the same spot as seen in the photograph above, this time taken in 1995. The cottages have been given a modern facelift but the old tree has survived reasonably well.

24. Another countryfied scene from the mid 1940s with Richard, Veronica and Jimmy Lucas leaving their smallholding at Cefn Coch for the village of Pentwyn.

25. A revival centenary ploughing match held at Church Farm Mynyddislwyn in 1972, it being the first time horses had been used for a number of years, left to right are Mr A Johns, Lou Davies, John Davies, Elwyn Davies and Harry Davies. In 1991, Lou Davies of Crumlin Farm won the Welsh Ploughing Championship at Abergele in North Wales.

26. Door to door deliveries of fresh milk direct from the farm are yet another thing of the past. Holding the horse, in the year 1900 is Helen Morgan with young Courtney on the cart. The family resided at Nantgoy Farm and are seen here on a daily round to Cwmnant and Aberbeeg.

27. Here is another example of a latter day home delivery service. This is Mr Jack Loynes delivering meat at the Old School Road Trinant in about 1935.

28./29. Pantglas Farm Trinant which is thought to have been built in 1865, is pictured here in about 1900. Below is an aerial view of the farm and its outbuilding taken in 1971. Although extensive renovations have taken place over the years, the original 16th century farmhouse can be seen on the right of the picture. Attached to this building can also be seen a tiny chapel which would have been used for clandestine worship amongst local villagers during the early days of non conformist religion in the district.

30./31. Reproduced from a fine painting by artist Obediah Hodges in 1927 is The Pentwyn Inn and Farm. Below, and probably more familiar to today's generation is the same scene as photographed during the 1960s.

PT.6. PENTWYN INN, PENTWYN TRINANT.

32./33.   The upper and lower photographs seen here were taken during the construction of Trinant Terrace. The building of any new housing in Trinant had been virtually dormant for some 40 years, following the end of the First World War in 1918 until the commencement of today's housing estate in the mid 1950s, the time when these pictures were taken.

34. Many local inhabitants may well remember the 'Prefabs'. These were pre-fabricated houses which were built throughout the country during the severe housing shortage following the end of the Second World War in 1945. At the time, it was intended that these buildings would have a life expectancy of 10 years maximum, but they proved to be very successful and in fact, in some areas, there were protestations from the occupants at having to move when the homes were dismantled. Those in Trinant were demolished in the 1970s to make way for new housing.

35. The Trinant and Cwmnant Social Centre pictured in 1971. First opened during the 1930s, the hall was a popular venue for concerts, dancing, flower shows and Youth Club meetings etc. Unfortunately the building was destroyed by fire in May 1975.

CHAPTER 2

Religious Matters

36. A rare photograph of the original Horeb Congregational Church which first opened its doors for prayers in the year 1829.

37./38. These are photographs of members of Horeb Sunday School from the days of much devotion by parents and children alike. Above, there are almost 100 teachers and pupils pictured outside the chapel in 1918. Below the year is approximately 1924 and a one-time traditional and very popular Sunday School walk is in progress.

39./40. These are some of the workers employed during the construction of 'New' Horeb Chapel in 1899/1900. Non conformist religious services were first held in Trinant in 1824, by small groups of locals meeting in an old house known as 'The Spout', near the old works and coal level. In 1825 it was decided to further the movement by building a chapel proper and in 1829 a deed was signed by a Mr Norman Protheroe of Newport who gave a piece of land 'Forever plus one day' for the sole purpose of building Horeb Chapel.

41.   The original chapel was to survive some 70 years before a more modern place of worship was built as seen in these two photographs. This new chapel was completed in 1901 on a plot of land just 20 yards from the old building and a small mortgage of £150 was required to complete it. The first Pastor of 'new' Horeb was the Rev James Thomas.

42.   An interior view of Horeb taken in 1995 and stood amongst the pews is the Rev Howell Mitchell, a native of Trinant and current Pastor of the Church. Rev Mitchell also manages to conduct services at a number of other local chapels whilst his daughter Helen, is the regular organist at Horeb. The chapel also provides a Sunday School for the children, in the very capable hands of Rev Mitchell, his wife Mary and Mrs Edwina Angel.

43./44. These two photographs are of Horeb Sunday School walks from 1927. The pioneer of a Sunday School at Horeb Chapel was a gentleman by the name of Mr Tom Jones who can be seen as the workman in the centre back of the photograph on page 28. Mr Jones was held in high esteem throughout a lifetime membership of Horeb, increasing his number of pupils to a total of 70 children from a first time class of just 8.

45. Following a school walk, the members, pupils and friends of Horeb relax and enjoy a little party in 1948. Services at the chapel were conducted entirely in Welsh until gentle persuasion brought the introduction of the English language in about 1875. The then minister, the Rev Thomas Lewis eventually succumbed and led the first English speaking service and thus the Welsh tongue disappeared permanently from the chapel.

46. The chapel's Sunday School walks continued to flourish as the years advanced and the photograph above was taken at an event in 1955. Hopefully, some of the youngsters pictured here, will be reading this book and recall their past Sunday School events.

47. Another very popular event provided for, by the chapels was the annual outing. Above is a group from Horeb Chapel enjoying themselves at Barry Island in the summer of 1939.

48. Children of Horeb Chapel Sunday School pose for a photograph in December 1925 and dressed as Father Christmas is Sam Bessant. To his right is Mrs A Holloway and left is Mrs A Jones, all three were dedicated Sunday School teachers.

49. The Wesleyan Methodist Church Trinant. This particular picture was taken shortly after its opening in 1901.

50. The Wesleyan Chapel walk in 1926. Methodists first met for worship in the Board Schools in 1894. Not satisfied for long with this arrangement local inhabitants took it upon themselves to build their own church. A local lady provided the site and as much stone from her land that might be needed.

51. These Wesleyan children are being led into song by Mrs Olwen Davies in 1948.

52. This is another photograph of the 1948 Sunday School Anniversary. Men and women alike toiled relentlessly to build this chapel at the end of the last century. A horse was purchased from some travelling gypsies, a cart and harness provided by a local farmer and the workers scoured the countryside in search of materials. The church was eventually completed in 1901 at a cost of £764 and could house a congregation of 200 souls.

53. This time the year is 1950 and the chapel members enjoy another celebratory walk around Trinant village. Local inhabitants will no doubt recognise a number of familiar faces appearing here.

54. Probably photographed in the mid 1950s is another group of Methodist worshippers of Trinant and district.

55. A new extension to the Wesleyan Chapel was completed in 1983 and here is a gathering to mark the event in July of that year. The building was officially opened by Councillor Bernard Cole seen with the key at the door and the ceremonial service was performed by the Reverend Tom Davies of Oakdale also to be seen on this photograph.

CHAPTER 3

Local Working Life

56. The Navigation Colliery Crumlin as it looked in 1912. This colliery was said to have a life expectancy to the year 2000, but that was not to be the case, as we know and it finally closed in September 1967.

The Miner

Every day the miner wakes
All his working clothes he takes
At the pithead he arrives
Underground all risk their lives

He shovels and shovels with all his might
He goes past day and into night
And when he goes to get his pay
He has to work another day

Lawrence Shapcott
Trinant Junior School, 1969

In Loving Memory

of the
3508 MINERS WHO LOST THEIR LIVES

COLLIERY DISASTERS

IN NORTH WALES, SOUTH WALES, AND MONMOUTHSHIRE DURING THE PAST 90 YEARS.

Date	Killed		Date	Killed
1837—May 10, Plas-yr-Argoed, Mold	21		1877—March 8, Worcester Pit, Swansea.	18
1837—June 17, Blaina (Mon.)	21		1878—September 1, Abercarn	62
1844—January 1, Dinas	12		1878—September 11, Abercarn	268
1845—August 2, Cwmbach	28		1879—January 13, Dinas	3
1846—January 14, Risca	35		1879—Sept. 22, Waunllwyd, Ebbw Vale.	84
1848—June 21, Victoria (Mon.)	11		1880—July 15, Risca	119
1849—Aug. 11, Letty Shenkin, Aberdare.	52		1880—Dec. 10, Naval Steam Colliery	96
1850—Dec. 14, New Duffryn Colliery	13		1882—January 15, Risca	4
1852—May 10, Duffryn	64		1882—February 11, Coedcae	6
1853—March 12, Risca Vale	10		1883—February 1, Coedcae	5
1856—July 13, Cymmer	114		1883—August 21, Gelli	4
1858—October 13, Duffryn	20		1884—January 16, Cwmavon	10
1859—April 5, Neath, Chain Colliery	26		1884—January 23, Penygraig	11
1860—December 1, Risca	146		1884—Nov. 8, Pochin Colliery, Tredegar.	14
1862—February 19, Gethin, Merthyr	47		1885—Naval Colliery	14
1863—October 17, Morgam	39		1885—December 24, Mardy	81
1863—December 24, Maesteg	14		1887—February 18, Ynysbir	37
1865—June 16, Tredegar	2		1888—May 14, Aber, Tynewydd	5
1865—December 20, Upper Gethin	30		1890—January 20, Glen Pit, Pontypool.	5
1867—November 8, Ferndale	178		1890—February 6, Llanerch	176
1869—May 23, Llanerch	7		1890—March 8, Morfa	87
1869—June 10, Ferndale	60		1892—August 12, Great Western Colliery	58
1870—July 23, Llanasmlet	19		1892—August 26, Park Slip	110
1871—February 24, Pentre	38		1894—June 25, Cilfynydd	276
1871—October 4, Gelli Pit, Aberdare	4		1896—January 28, Tylorstown	57
1872—Jan. 10, Oakwood, Llynvi Valley.	11		1899—August 18, Llest Colliery, Garw.	19
1872—March 2, Victoria	19		1901—May 24, Sengenhydd	82
1872—March 8, Wernfach	18		1901—September 10, Llanbradach	12
1874—April 5, Abertillery	6		1905—March 10, Clydach Vale	31
1874—July 24, Charles Pit, Llansamlet.	19		1905—July 5, Wattstown	119
1875—December 4, New Tredegar	22		1913—October 13, Senghenydd	436
1875—December 6, Llan Pit, Pentyrch	12		1923—April 26, Trimsaron	9
1876—December 13, Abertillery	20		1927—March 1, Cwm, Ebbw Vale	52

A sudden change; at God's command they fell:
They had no chance to bid their friends farewell;
Swift came the blast, without a warning given,
And bid them haste to meet their God in Heaven.

57. Above is a painful reminder of the true price of coal and a former advertisement from Philip Taylor Ltd.

58. A Crumlin Miners Rescue Team in 1916. The rescue station for the instruction of miners to engage in rescue work in the mines was built in 1910 by the Monmouthshire Colliers Rescue Association.

59. A surviving photograph of the Millbrook Level in 1912 which was owned by Mr Ivor Edwards. In the photograph left to right are Henry Richards and Sidney Walters. This level was originally opened by the Millbrook Coal Co. of Newport and operated for about 40 years until the 1920s.

60./61. At one time the hills of Trinant were littered with privately owned coal levels, a number of which were producing coal until the 1970s. These two photographs show some local lads filling their tin baths during the destitute years of the 1920s. At the Mount Pleasant level the two gentlemen standing are, left Phillip Norris and right Tom Kibby.

62. Here are some workers pictured at the Graig levels during the Great General Strike of 1926. The Welsh valleys were hit particularly hard during the 1920s and 1930s and none more so than the miners themselves with continual confrontation with the coal owners in the struggle for a living wage.

63. A scene from a coal level at the Kendon in about 1911. On the far right is Mr Tom Buckley the local blacksmith calling to shoe the horses. It is unusual however, as to be seen in the picture, for a donkey to be employed underground. Tom Buckley was a renowned one-mile runner throughout the valleys, accumulating an array of trophies during his lifetime.

64. On the local mountainside some members of the Ware family pose for a photograph among the levels during the 1926 Strike. As a matter of utter survival, men, women and children were forced to scour the waste tips in search of fuel to keep their home fires burning.

65. Sam and Nancy Topliss. Mr Topliss started work in the mines in 1890. He retired from The Navigation Colliery at Crumlin in 1950 at the age of 72. Sam is pictured here displaying his certificate from The National Coal Board in recognition of his long and loyal service to the industry and with it he received the princely sum of £5.

66. Mr D Evans, General Secretary of the NUM presenting a cheque to Mr Bill Clayton on behalf of Crumlin Navigation Workmens' Fund to mark his retirement from the Navigation Colliery in 1955. Also in the photograph is Mr S Gulliford, Crumlin Lodge Secretary and Mr T Leader, Crumlin Lodge Chairman.

67./68. Ton-Tyr-Bel Level Trinant was opened by Mr Lyndon Robinson in 1952 and closed in 1978. In both photographs is seen Mr Ron Matthews guiding a tram of coal being hauled by 'Darkie' his faithful horse.

69./70. Both of these photographs feature the Jones family, owners of The Rosemont Level. On the left, pictured in 1960 is Rose Cottage at Kendon, the family abode. Right, is a scene from a typical working day at Rosemont and to be seen are Ron, Dennis and Emlyn Jones with their work horse 'Trixie'.

PENTWYN AND DISTRICT AUTO CLUB
present the

East South Wales Centre Championship

SCRAMBLE

SOLO AND SIDECAR

Pentwyn Course, TRINANT
Near Crumlin, Mon.
(By kind permission of Mrs. G. Robinson)

SUNDAY, 21st AUGUST, 1966
FIRST EVENT AT 2.30 P.M.

Official Programme 3/-

71.   A five minute break is allowed for this photograph at Rosemont. On this occasion we see Dennis Jones, Howard Hiley, Colin Ricketts, Ron Jones and of course 'Trixie'.

72.   This is another rescue team pictured at Crumlin in the 1920s. Amongst the men's breathing apparatus, in the front, can be seen a revival box. This was used for the reviving of a semi concious canary which would have been used underground in the detection of the dreaded gas.

73.   This is a photograph taken in the canteen of the Aberbeeg South and Navigation Collieries to mark the retirement of a number of fellow miners. Those retiring after many years service are seated in the front row and left to right they are: Frank Taylor, Harry Haines, Fred Cook, Chris Roberts, Arthur Powell, Ted Gifford and Jack Vigers. Other faces to be seen are Mr W Short (Colliery Manager), Mr J Williamson (Under Manager), Mr Golding (Area Agent), and Ada Nash (Canteen Manageress).

74.   Crumlin Mines Rescue Instructors 1986. Left to right are Roy Griffiths, Bernard Watkins, Jack Toomer, Alan Howie (Superintendent), Bob Griffiths, Steven Nichols and Alistair Rennie.

75. A scene from the Gordon Colliery in about 1950 and on the left is Arthur Williams, Gordon Williams is the young lad and on the right is Lionel Williams, the founder of the original Gordon Colliery Company.

76. Another day at the Gordon Colliery with the young lad Wayne Davies and 'Bright' the horse.

The Gordon Colliery

The Gordon Colliery was a vision come true for local miner Lionel Williams. Working during his youth at nearby Millbrook Colliery, Mr Williams had long dreamed of one day owning his own coal mine and had always suspected that a rich untapped seam of coal existed near his cottage at Trinant. He resolved to find this 'Bounty' lying beneath the ground and after much discussion with wife Doris, decided to invest their meagre life savings in the project. The year was 1945, the war was over and the cry for coal was intense. A 14 year lease was granted by the Pontypool Park Estate in August of that year and so followed nearly 12 months of strenuous manual labour for Lionel. His only implements were a pick, a shovel and the constant companionship of his 7 year old son Gordon, thus the name 'Gordon Colliery' was adopted and registered as a company as such. The 'Black Gold' was finally struck in the summer of 1946, after some 36 yards of tunnelling and the reward was rich. The Mynyddislwyn seam, which had been ignored since the 1880s had been reached and first estimates revealed a staggering 20 year supply of available top quality coal. This was a golden era for the coal industry and demand quickly outstripped supply at Gordon. From the beginnings of 60 tons per week with just 2 or 3 men working, within months, output trebled with 16 men employed with a drover and horses pulling trams from morning to night.

The quality of the coal mined at Gordon was exceptionally high, with a particularly low ash content, which led to contracts being won to supply the electricity industry and even overseas customers. The peak of the operation was probably reached in the 1960s with the Gordon Co. expanding so, to gain control of numerous other local mines such as Bush Level, Pentwyn Coals and Rassau Mines. What was 20 years before, a one-man operation, now employed 45 staff, with many of the Williams family fully involved and what appeared to be a never ending supply of coal from the hills of Trinant. Then as the 1970s began, so did the demand for coal as a domestic fuel, subside at breakneck speed, with newly discovered North Sea Gas becoming the fuel of the future. The original mine closed in 1972 but son Gordon continued to operate as a coal merchant from his home, Garw Wen Farm until his untimely death in 1984 at the age of 45. The story of Gordon Colliery is a classic example of how one man with a dream and a little initiative can turn out to be the local entrepreneur.

77. Abercarn Urban District Council Election held at Trinant School in 1932. Most of the gentlemen can be named and they are, left to right, John Thomas, Unknown, Dai Jones, Unknown, Richard Jones, George Beach, Unknown, William Harris, Charles Skuse, Walter Smith, Francis Morrisey, Chris Evans and Bill Skuse.

78. It is 1948 and the very active ladies section of the Trinant Labour Party willingly pose for a photograph. Some faces to be recognised, left to right are, back row: Unknown, K Thomas, J Davies, Mrs Evans, E Jarrett, V Harvey, D Carpenter, A Holloway, H Jenkins and M Daniels. Middle row: A Perry, M Morgan, S Smith and A Smith. Front row: C Richards, G Evans, M Perry, I Hiley and D Foxwell.

Local Personalities

79./80. Here is a 'mature' local of Trinant, Mr Cliff Bessant, seen on the left during his early army days. Mr Bessant joined the forces in 1935 at the age of eighteen, with the 3rd Dragoon Guards, Carabiniers and served in the North West Frontier, India from 1936 until 1944. He returned to Europe in 1944, being transferred to the 8th Royal Irish Hussars in preparation for the 'D' Day landings in June of that year. Spending some 23 years in the army, he eventually retired as Sergeant Major and ultimately sought residence at the Royal Chelsea Hospital. The photograph below shows him in uniform being presented to the Duchess of Kent at the Hospital during an annual 'Founders Day', parade in June 1994.

81. Seen here is another Trinant 'Old Soldier', Albert Clayton. He was working at Oakdale Colliery before the outbreak of war in 1939, coalmining being a 'reserved occupation' at the time and not subject to the call-up regulations. However, Albert decided to volunteer his services for the country and joined the Welsh Guards in July 1939, two months before war was declared. However, after less than a year's service, in June 1940, he was caught up in the debacle at Dunkirk and was taken prisoner whilst fighting a rear guard action at West Cappel, France. This was the start of a nightmare, commencing with the infamous forced march for hundreds of miles across Europe. Albert eventually ended up at Stalag 8 B Lamsdorf in Poland where he was to spend almost 5 years as a prisoner of war, before the camp was eventually liberated by the Allies in April 1945. After his demob and homecoming to the United Kingdom, he returned to his original occupation in the mines. Albert Clayton passed away in 1992 at the age of 75.

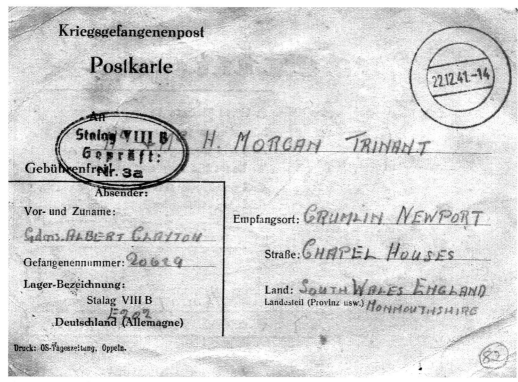

82. Above is a 'Kriegsgefangenenpost' card used for prisoner of war messages out of Germany. This one, sent in December 1941 is from Albert Clayton to his sister, Mrs Morgan at Trinant and would have taken anything from 3 to 6 months to arrive at its destination, usually via the Red Cross organisation in Switzerland.

83. The Cenotaph at Horeb Chapel Trinant. The names of eight fallen heroes from World War I are to be seen at the top of the memorial and a further seven victims of the 1939-45 War are named on the additional plaque below.

84. On the left is an unsung hero of Trinant, Ron Smith. Ron's experiences of action in World War II make interesting conversation. In the desert campaign of North Africa he received several bullet wounds to the back and neck which put him out of action for a while. Not content with that and whilst an anti-tank gunner with the 6th Battalion, Green Howards, he was amongst the first wave of troops to land on the beaches of Normandy on 6th June 1944. Within an hour of landing he was caught in an explosion suffering severe leg injuries and lay wounded on the beach for 25 hours before being transferred to a hospital ship. His life was saved by the brilliant surgeons at a Birmingham Hospital, but unfortunately he lost his lower right leg due to the severity of his injuries. This has never deterred Ron Smith and he has since revisited France to honour former comrades of those dark days.

85. Some members of the 2nd Monmouthshire Territorial Army at one of their summer camps in about 1938, shortly before they were to see active service at the outbreak of World War II. Just one of the boys' names is known on this occasion that of George Williams sat in the centre of the front row, he later served with the RAF.

86. Here we see another wartime photograph, this time of Trinant local, John Clayton sat upon a 1940's Norton motorcycle. He was a despatch rider for the Trinant Home Guard prior to service in the RAF.

87. This is a smiling Trinant lady smartly dressed in Eastern attire who will be recognised as Diane Jones. Diane initially qualified as a nursing midwife but went on to become a missionary at the Sunshine Leprosy Hospital, Nepal. She also spent much of her valuable time giving help to the needy population in the more remote parts of that distant country. The lady, now married and still nursing, resides even further afield in New Zealand and it is hoped she will come by a copy of this Trinant book to remind her of her native land of Wales.

88. This is an outward bound photograph of some junior Trinant personalities in about 1930 and to be seen are: back row, left to right, Dorothy Smith, Cliff Bessant, George Davies, Dennis Clayton, Reg Weybourne, Ron Smith, Horace Daniels, Albert Clayton, Jack Weybourne, Jimmy Donald, Sam Beach, Edwina Watts, Martha Morgan, Cora Evans and Edna Smith. Middle row: Noreen Holloway, Melvyn Phillips, William Price, Eric Price, Ken Smith, Idris Smith, Mervyn Smith, John Jones, Dennis Smith, Ron Lewis, George Lewis and Bertha Richards. Front row: Cyril Smith, Cliff Smith, Bernard Phillips, Billy Holyfield, Billy Williams, Jim Smith, Vivian Rowley, Dennis Holyfield, Ken Morrisey, Keith Jenkins, Billy Rowley, Chris Holding, Frank Holding, Jack Holyfield and Megan Smith.

89. Here's a local character whom some readers may well remember, George Williams or 'George Sam', as he was more familiarly known. This particular photograph was taken during the 1940s and he is sat on his chair posing with a badger. George was a Trinant farm labourer who was usually to be sighted early in the morning, accompanied by his terrier dogs, going fox hunting on behalf of the local farmers who would graciously reward his efforts. It was said of George Sam that he had a better sense of smell than the fox and had a unique skill of being able to outwit the animal.

90. Some of the local boys stop for a photograph on their way to Pen-y-Fan Pond. Left to right are T Edwards, Unknown, J Lewis, A Bridges, I Jones and D Phillips. Judging by the fashion of the young mens' headgear, the photograph probably dates from about 1920.

91. Trinant St John's Ambulance 1945. Back row standing, left to right are Mark Davies, Glyn Morrisey, Raymond Smith, Roy Carpenter, Elvet Morrisey, Clive Daniels, Penry Davies, Haydn Rees, Raymond Holding and Douglas Padfield. Middle row: Howell Mitchell, Malcolm Ricketts, Supt. Mr David Ashford, Dr Kurt Trigger, Henry Rowley and Haydn Morgan. Front row: Emlyn Taylor, Glyn Morgan and Lewis Taylor.

92. Trinant St John's Ambulance 1949. Left to right, back row, Officer Glyn Morgan, Jimmy Lucas, Garnet Davies, Leo Davies, Raymond Holding, Howell Jenkins, Haydn Rees, Haydn Morgan and Supt. David Ashford. Front row: Phillip Jones, Barry Mitchell, Michael Rees and Douglas Padfield.

93. From the 1930s these ladies of the local youth club are enjoying a short break at Dimland, Llantwit Major. Among the many faces are: Dilys Richardson, Maisie Weybourne, Winnie Smith, Eileen Williams and Iris Morgan.

94. This is another group of ladies, this time the schoolgirls of Trinant and Crumlin are enjoying a summer holiday at Ogmore. These Summer Camps were extremely popular with the younger generation before the last war. Some of the smiling faces belong to: Miss Gwyneth Holyfield Schoolteacher, Doreen Smith, Gwyneth Rees, Thelma Thomas, Iris Price, Doreen Weybourne, Doreen Daniels and Betty Smith.

95. This is a period photograph from about 1909 of some Trinant lads. The mode of dress is a little unusual, to say nothing of the solid tyred bicycle. On the far right is Mr William (Barber) Thomas and second from the left is David Bessant. Sadly, not too many years after this picture was taken, David Bessant was killed during the first World War at the infamous 'Hill 60' slaughter in Belgium. His name will be seen on the War Memorial on page 51.

96. The people of Trinant gather at the Trinant and Cwmnant Social Centre for the retirement of Mrs Nora Rowlands in 1948. Mrs Rowlands was a teacher at Trinant Board School for an amazing 50 years between 1898 and 1948 and is remembered for the exceptional accomplishment of teaching three generations of some local families.

97. Ernest Cox and his wife Florence standing on the door of their shop and post office in the late 1950s. This is still the site of the current post office managed by Mr and Mrs Tovey.

98. Mr Tom Jones, stonemason. It was he who innaugurated the Sunday School at Horeb Chapel in 1875, with a class of only seven or eight pupils. So with two other colleagues they canvassed the district so well that the attendance soon reached seventy plus. Mr Jones was also the stonemason who worked on the building of the present Horeb Chapel.

99. On the left is Mrs Sarah Ann Bessant who was the daughter of Mr Tom Jones as seen in photograph No 98. Mrs Bessant was the well known local midwife who did her training whilst her own young family grew up during the early years of this century. Whilst trained specifically in midwifery at Bristol University, the locals of Trinant soon respected her nursing skills and would turn to her on many an occasion for help and medical advice when needed most. Her task as the local midwife was not easy, there being no telephone service in the vicinity for instance. Her practice was known to cover a widespread area and visits to her patients would be carried out on foot through all weathers and conditions. On numerous occasions it was neccessary for would-be fathers to knock upon her door in the middle of the night and escort Nurse Bessant to the expectant mother some distance away. She eventually retired after 25 years service, in May 1938 and as a mark of their appreciation of her work, the villagers presented her with an inscribed clock at a special ceremony held in the Social Centre. Sarah Ann Bessant died in 1960 at the ripe old age of 84.

100./101. From some years ago is this photograph taken at Pen Coed Cae Farm which was near the Pen-y-Fan Pond. Pictured at the farm gate with his dog is Mr Ivor Evans, whom many locals may well remember. Below, and to illustrate yet another example of the process of change, is the same area as it appears today, hardly recognisable perhaps. The old farm buildings have virtually given way to a most modern dwelling, bearing little resemblance to the original 19th century construction.

102. A meeting of Trinant Senior Citizens at the Social Centre in 1955 and to be seen are: Mr & Mrs E Jones, Mr & Mrs C Davies, Mr & Mrs P Davies, Mrs M Morgan, Mrs F Vigers, Mrs M Few, Mrs K Thomas, Mrs Shaw, Mrs P Lovell, Miss G Jones, Mrs C Morgan, Mrs M Watts, Mrs A Kibby, Mr B Jones, Mr W Bessant, Mr S Bessant, Mr L Williams, Mr M Williams and Councillor Mr I Jarrett.

103. The Social Centre sets the scene for this group photograph, celebrating the 80th birthday of Mrs Amy Kibby in 1957. The event was attended by many friends and relatives as pictured here.

104. County Councillor Mr I Jarrett making a presentation to Mrs B I Morgan in 1957, leaving after teaching at Trinant School for 30 years. Also in the photograph are Councillor Mr A England and Headmaster Mr E Finney.

105. Some 'regulars' perhaps, pictured outside The Pentwyn Inn during the 1930s and left to right they are, Lou Jones, Fred Tucker, Charlie Davies and Jim Jones. Fred Tucker is the son of John Tucker seen outside his post office on page 16 of this book.

106. Pentwyn Inn 1920. Left to right are John (Henry) Davies, Tom Morris, Annie Beach, Elsie Arnold, Unknown, Unknown, Mrs Probert and daughter and George Thomas. At the time when this picture was taken, a large field stood behind the Inn, which was a most popular venue for many local sporting events including even horse racing.

107. Again, taken at the rear of the Pentwyn Inn is this group and noting the presence of guns and working dogs, the men are probably preparing for a day's local 'Shoot'. Back row, left to right are: Will Price, Tom Smith, Charlie Bessant, Lou Jones, Chris Evans, Charlie Davies, Annie Morgan, Dai Thomas and Ike Rees.

CHAPTER 5

Sport & Entertainment

108. The Trinant Carnival held to mark the Festival of Britain in 1951. The crowd here are pictured in the Square awaiting the crowning of the Carnival Queen. Some familiar faces to be seen are: Harry & Neville Coombes, Ray Kimber, Jean Davies, Glenys Clayton, Ruby & Ken Williams, George & Penelope Williams, Joyce Thomas, Edwin Phillips, Doreen Smith, Edwina Morrisey, Mike Rees, Rhodwen Jenkins, Mair Jenkins, Eirwen Smith, Bronwen Evans, Dilys Smith, May Lucas, Marlene James, Enid Phillips, Raymond Smith, Jimmy & Anthony Beach, Pearl Gardiner, Glyn Morgan, Haydn Morgan, Audrey Rees and Dennis Jones.

109. A carnival celebrating the 1937 Coronation. Back row, left to right are Thelma Thomas, Mary Morris, Ceridwen Thomas (as Britannia), Winnie Rees, Doreen Daniels. Front row: Betty Jones, Thelda Rees, Clive Williams (as the King), John Gregory, Betty Smith (as the Queen), Pamela Rowley and Ceinwen Richards.

110. The Festival of Britain Carnival 1951 and Carnival Queen June Williams is being crowned by Olwen Davies with Councillor Idris Jarrett. Also to be seen are Jill Holyfield, Cynthia Smith, Barry Mitchell, Judith Hyde, Carol Williams, Carol Jones, Christine Goodwin, Roger Kimber and Colin Brimfield.

111. In Trinant Square during the summer of 1952 is another village carnival. The Carnival Queen in the centre is Rhodwen Jenkins together with her entourage of local girls.

112. This is another carnival at Trinant held to celebrate the coronation of Queen Elizabeth II in June 1953. The Carnival Queen here is Barbara Carpenter and Mrs Verley Stevens, playing the part of the Queen Mother with some children to be recognised as: Gloria Hyde, Denise Stevens, Judith Hyde, Carol Harwood, Dennis Hodder, Edwina Jones, Unknown and Michael Morgan.

113. Above is a carnival picture from about 1920. The participants in their competitive costumes are all local inhabitants of that time but unfortunately the author has not been able to trace any of their names on this occasion.

114. Some of the characters in a carnival at Trinant during the early 1950s are Mrs E Jarrett, Mrs D Davies, Mrs E Padfield, Mrs E Morrisey, Mrs J Davies, Unknown, Miss V Jarrett, Mrs N Ricketts and Miss J Phillips.

115. Miss Mair Jenkins, secretary of the Trinant Girls Youth Club presents Mr Idris Jarrett secretary of Trinant and Cwmnant Social Centre with money raised by the girls club for a new piano in 1948.

116. Some of the Trinant Girls Youth Club with Girl Guides from other parts of the county at a summer camp at Llangorse Lake in 1949.

117. The Betty Cox Dancing Troupe 1952. Back row, left to right, Betty Weybourne, Rita Weybourne, Anita Smith, Judy Watkins, Maureen Smith, Lavinia Beach, Cynthia Smith, Jacqueline Hardacre, Sandra Payne, Pat Clayton and Kath Rees.

118. Trinant Brownies circa 1967. Back row, left to right, Jacqueline Perkins, Ruby Garland and Virgina Roseblade. Second row: Tina Garland, Kerry Knight, Susan Woodford, Christine Mitchell, Linda Jones, Stephanie Roseblade and Susan Bishop. Third row: Jacqueline Padmore, Mandy Woodford, Dawn Jenkins, Caroline Studholme, Susan Edwards, Paula Mitchell and Ann Williams. Front row: Sharon Bevan, Mandy Oliver, Margaret Studholme, Denise Haines, Kim Jones, Julie Bishop and Andrea Perkins.

119. Members and Judges at the Trinant and Cwmnant Horticultural Show 1949. Back row, left to right, Mrs I Jefferies, Mrs H Morrisey, Mrs O Davies, Mr B Thomas, Mrs F Vigers, Mr T Evans, Mrs J Davies, Mrs C Jones, Mrs K Thomas and Mrs G Evans. Second row: Mr I Jarrett, Mr R Thatcher, Mr P Davies, Mr E Daniels, Unknown, Mr B Grubb and Unknown.

120. Taken in 1987/88 in the Islwyn Council Chambers at Pontllanfraith, this picture is of a group of ladies belonging to the Trinant and Cwmnant Craft Class with Mayor of the Borough, Mr Fred Perkins. The ladies present are, back row, left to right, Rene Barugh, Lesley Pritchard, Andrea De Place, Jenny Todd, Ginny Davies, Gwyneth Evans and Mair Holyfield. Front row: Annette Fender, Mary Smith, Leah Robinson, Angela Davies, Dilys Robinson, Jennifer Vesey and Ethel Padfield.

121. Dressed up for the Sunday School Christmas Concert 1925 are, left to right, Bronwen Skuse, Eunice Morgan, Marion McNeil, Rachel Price, Bertha Jones, Moffryd Davies and Netta Waites.

122. Again, dressed for the same concert as above are the local boys who are, left to right, Emrys Daniels, Haydn Daniels, John Cawley, Gwyn Thomas, Eric Price, John Jones, Jim Donald, Billy Price and Idris Smith.

123. Trinant Jazz Band 1950. Back row, left to right, Lilian Scott, Peggy Morgan, Dilys Smith, Moria Thomas, Evelyn Golding, Terry Robinson, Peggy Harwood and Olive Hyde. Front row: George Hodder, Edwina Morrisey, Audrey Rees, Margaret Jarrett, Joyce Johns, Thora Hodder and Selwyn Hyde.

124. Trinant Jazz Band 1953. Back row, left to right, Barry Mitchell, George Hardacre, Rodney Payne, Tony Smith, Keith Scott, Terry Beddis, Michael Rees, Alan Bowditch, Glyn Matthews, Albert Clayton, John Hodder and Malcolm Smith. Front row: Graham Clayton, Lyndon Lloyd, Ralph Thomas, Martin Clayton and Donald Morgan.

125. These day-trippers are pictured during the early 1950s whilst on an excursion to Tenby organised from the Social Centre. Among those pictured are, Mr & Mrs H Morgan, Mr & Mrs J Poletti, Mr & Mrs D Smith, Mr & Mrs J Lloyd, Mr & Mrs E Jones, Mr & Mrs F Padfield, Mr J Watts, Mr R Watts, Mr W Jones, Mrs C Jones, Mrs E Gardiner, Pearl & John Gardiner, Cynthia & Meryl Smith, Terry Jones, Haydn Morgan, Douglas Padfield and Glenys Clayton.

126. Children of the employees of Golden Wonder, Croespenmaen enjoying a fun day with athletic stars Colin Jackson, Fatima Whitbread, Sally Gunnell and Roger Black.

127. Enjoying a picnic at Pen-y-Fan Pond in early 1940. Left to right are Jack Kibby, Unknown, Olwen Kibby, Marion Kibby, Tom Kibby, Peggy Kibby, George Kibby, Rose Kibby, Harry Kibby and Marion Rees

128. Pen-y-Fan Pond and this photograph was taken during the winter of 1947. Left to right are Henry Rowley, Phillip Addis, Brenda Holyfield, Cyril Morgan and Brian Holyfield.

129. Llewyncelin Male Voice Choir Trinant circa 1929 with Conductor Lewis Williams. Some of the members seen here include, John Thomas, Ernest Daniels, Bill Williams, Percy Williams, Francis Morrisey, Charlie Thomas, Bill Jones, Jack Vigers, Dai Williams, Bill Shepherd and Billy (George) Jones.

130./131. This is Victory in Europe Day as it really happened in May 1945 and here are views of the Pentwyn Road 'Street Party', held to rejoice at the cessation of nearly 6 years of war.

132. VE Day, May 8th 1995 was the occasion to celebrate 50 years of peace in Europe. Parties were held throughout the land and these two scenes are of the residents of Trinant Terrace marking the event.

133. Some of the partygoers, suitably dressed for the occasion are: - Back row, left to right, Jamie Baine, Carly Price, Denise Price and Unknown. Middle row: Christopher Snooks, Jean Snooks, Myra Leader, Jenny Daniels, Luke Bodman, Jeanette Madden, Kirsty Bodman, Maureen Rees, Siân Daniels, Lynn Bates and Veronica Davies. Front row: Joan Smith, Chris Tudgay, Gillian James, Maureen Evans, Winnie Hayward, Carol Smith, Mair Pike and Lauren Webley.

134. The auburn haired Haydn Morgan, Trinant's rugby hero, whose speed was a midfield menace to outside halves on the rugby pitch. He gained his first international cap against England in 1958 and went on to win 27 caps in total. As a specialised breakaway forward, his other achievements included a Monmouthshire County Cap, Army Cap, an Irish Wolfhound and Vice Captain for the Barbarians and British Lions. It was Haydn and England's Derek Morgan who scored the tries for the Barbarians which enabled them to become the only side to beat the Springboks on their British Tour in 1961. Rugby fans will also recall that with Alan Pask and John Lewis, he formed the most famous back row that Abertillery ever produced. Nicknamed the Red Devil for his love of red jerseys and matching hair, Haydn Morgan became a household name in Australia, New Zealand, South Africa and Fiji. Haydn eventually settled in South Africa where he lives with his family to this day.

135. Trinant RFC 1923-4. Back row, left to right, W Rowley (Treasurer), T Morgan (Vice Captain), W Norris (Vice Chairman), E Rowley, H Porter, B Davies, A Morrissey, W Smith, D Porter and S Holloway. Middle row: L Rowley, L. Jones, W Thomas, J Price, D Jones (Captain), Unknown, H Rowley, J Thomas. Front row: J Preece, I Thomas and G Skuse.

136. Trinant RFC 1956. Back row, left to right, Ray Morgan, Dennis Smith, Peter Richards, Warren Williams, David Davies, Mike Rees, Harry Rowley, John Beckett, Howard Seabourne, Lou Ricketts, Ray Holding and Windsor Rees. Middle row: Alan Jones, Glyn Morgan, Ian Smith, Harry Davies, Jim Smith, Haydn Rees, Colin Ricketts and Reg Weybourne. Front row: Ken Smith and Gwyn Jones.

137. Trinant RFC 1957. Back row, left to right, Glyn Morrisey, Colin Ricketts, Haydn Rees, Harry Rowley, Mike Rees, Trevor Parker, Garnet Davies, Gwyn Jones, Digger Smith, Horace Beach, Albert Clayton and Ray Morgan. Front row: Jim Smith, Howell Jenkins, Glyn Morgan, David Davies, Leo Davies, Ian Smith and Alan Jones.

138. Trinant RFC 1990. Back row, left to right, Brian Parfitt, Martin Clayton, Michael Parfitt, Jeff Relf, Dean Parfitt, Anthony Way, Martin Smith, Larry Haines, David Haines, Vivian Haines, Richard Bruten, Richard Rees, Steve Shepherd and Gavin Rogers. Front row: Christopher Way, Tony Price, Tony Lewis, Robert Rees (Captain), Simon Thomas, Mark Dixon and Steve Connett.

My Dad
My dad, Robert he's called
He's going a little bald
In his rugby he loves to be
Trying to kick penalties
He plays for Trinant with such pride
That one day he might score a try

He does a coupon every week
His fortune he is out to seek
He dreams and dreams every day
Of that big win that will come his way
I know he's bald and his dreams are mad
But I still love my dear old dad

Stacey Rees
Aged Eight

139. The Gelli Farm Trinant is the scene of a motorcycle scrambles event held by the Pentwyn and District Auto Club in 1966.

140. Pen-y-Fan Rangers AFC 1928. Back row, left to right, Phillip Norris, Charlie Kibby, Horace Thatcher, Clifford Hale, Billy Rose, Tom Sayers, Trevor Hale and Unknown. Middle row: Stan Evans, Ted Twissel, Reg Davies, Fred Watkins, Trevor Friend and Jack Thatcher. Front row: Dai Parson and Bob Larkin.

141. Pen-y-Fan Rangers AFC circa 1930. Back row, left to right are Stan Evans, Mr Baker, Reg Thatcher, Harold Tucker and Unknown. Second row: Will Thatcher, Billy Rose, Unknown, Cliff Hale and Mr S Evan (Senior). Front row: Bob Larkin, Charlie Kibby, Reg Davies and Wilf Davies.

142. Cwmnant Junior Football Team 1931-32. Standing, left to right, Mr Tucker, Mr Parson, Stan Evans, Unknown, Billy Lloyd, Unknown, Unknown, Unknown, Dai Parson, Ivor Trimm, Percy Davies and Jim Parson. Sitting: Unknown, Unknown, Wilf Davies, Unknown and Ted Parson.

144. Trinant Junior School Soccer Team 1965-66. Back row, left to right, Teacher Mr Parker, Paul Whitlock, Paul Gregory, Nigel Hockey, Graham Phillips, Jeffrey Lloyd, John Powell and Headmaster Mr Finney. Front row: Maldwyn Lovell, Stephen Daniels, Kerrison Thomas, Martin Snooks and Shane Walker.

144. Trinant Junior School Soccer Team 1977. Back row, left to right, Martin Phelps, Lee Daniels, Paul Davies, Phillip Easley, Robert Davies and Anthony Lewis. Front row: Steve Randall, Stephen Dee, Simon Thomas, Anthony Jones and Adam Summers.

145. Trinant Junior Soccer Team 1980. Back row, left to right, Charlie Davies, Archie Self and Philip James. Back row: Simon Evans, Robert Brown, Keith Davies, Ian James, Dean James, David Jenkins, Andrew Thomas and Matthew Veal. Front row: Andrew Jones, Gary Rogers, John Paul Haines, Ian Beckett, Nickie Haines, Andrew Rees, Simon Sterry and Dean Pullin.

146. This is a family photograph with a difference from the 1930s. Virtually all of the players in this cricket team are related in one way or another and formed their own team to challenge other local clubs particularly for charitable causes. Back row, left to right, Ivor Savery, Will Holyfield, Percy Holyfield and Sam Holyfield. Second row: Bill Townsend, Ivor Griffiths, Ron Boots and Tom Holyfield. Front row: Gwyn Parry, Jim Green, Alf Bessant, Dan Addis and Abe Green.

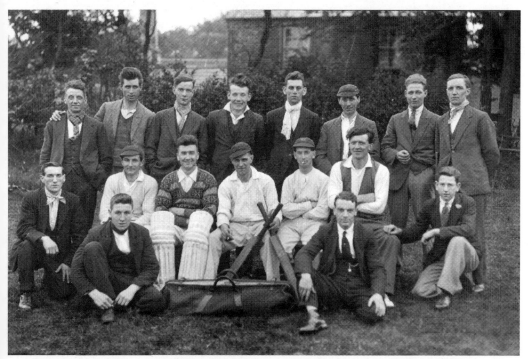

147. Trinant Cricket Team circa. 1930. Back row, left to right, Tom Smith, Tom Jones, Bill Bessant, Llewelyn Thomas, Wyndham Price, Tom Evans, Reg Morrisey and Joe Smith. Second row: Dai Davies, Harry Skuse, Elwin Thomas, Francis Morrisey, Dai Price, Norman Jenkins and Gwyn Price. Front row, Dick Phelps and Richard Jones.

148. Another sporting hero of the district was Dan Phillips of Cwmnant. He was a member of Newport Harriers and excelled as a cross country runner. His name will be found in The Guinness Book of Records participating in many International Championship events, heading the list with 14 appearances representing Wales between 1922 and 1937.

149. On the right is Sara Morgan, a Trinant resident pictured with her Welsh Cap which she won in 1991 whilst a member of the Welsh Ladies Rugby Team. This was the year of the first ever Womens' Rugby World Cup and Sara, as scrum half, achieved a debut try in the game against Sweden. Ladies rugby appears to have started in the district with a Blaenau Gwent team in 1986, their first fixture being against Swansea Uplands RFC and playing in this match was to give Sara's acquired taste for the sport. She was also captain of the Welsh Counties Ladies Rugby Team during the 1993/94 season.

150. A photograph taken at Gelli Farm 1907. George Sayers and Ernest Daniels shape up for a few rounds of boxing and looking on are their seconds Tom Phillips and Jack Morrisey (Senior).

151. Trinant combined darts and rugby team with trophies for the season 1967/68. The photograph was taken at Trinant Sports and Social Club and there are many familiar faces to be recognised.

CHAPTER 6

Schooldays

152. Trinant School Standard V, VI, VII 1925. Back row, left to right, Lucy Newman, Dolly Morrisey, Emma Ware, Vera Kurnock, Evelyn Hale, Enid Kurnock, Flossie Long, Louise Gwilliam, Hetty Scarrott, Rachel Price and Cyril Jones. Second row: Teacher Ossie Morris, Doris Thomas, Mary Daniels, Phyllis Tucker, Eunice Clayton, Iris Mead, Annie Waite, Phyllis Davies, Phyllis Morgan, Phyllis Thomas and Winnie Mapp. Third row: Jack Jones, Jack Holyfield, Percy Holyfield, Horace Thatcher, Harry Kibby, Jim Preece, Percy Davies, Jim Lawrence, Cyril Parson and Jim Shepherd. Front row: Monty Nash, Sam Holyfield, Roy Weybourne, Richard Phelps, Rhys Rees, Godfrey Bessant, Unknown, Jim Corbett, Harold Grey, George Williams and Russell Williams.

153. Trinant School Third and Babies 1925. Back row, left to right, Teacher Miss Pontin, Ivy Williams, Howard Skuse, Ken Smith, Aubrey Davies, Haydn Morgan, Wilf Hale, Arthur Trimm, Jimmy Donald and Rowley Jones. Middle row: Olga Blackwell, Henry Davies, Jimmy Beach, Edna Smith, Edwina Watts, Cora Evans, Billy Williams, John Cawley, Idris Smith, Vernon Parsons and Phyllis Smith. Front row: Winnie Thomas, Iris Morgan, Dorothy McNeil, Roy Thomas, Leslie Daniels, Horace Daniels, Thomas Daniels, Ben Morgan, Connie Jones, Ron Lewis and Mervyn Smith.

154. Trinant School Class VII 1946. Back row, left to right, Headmaster Mr George, Roy Boucher, Ken Harvey, Billy Jones, Lawrence Price, David Davies, Ray Smith and Teacher Mr Thomas. Front row: Glyn Morrisey, Glyn Morgan, Vivian Waters, Dorothy Gardiner, Jenny Smith, Nora Wilcox, Jean Addis, Barbara Williams, Gwyn Jones, Mark Davies and Edwin Williams.

155. Trinant School First Class and Infants 1946. Teacher Miss Purnell. Back row, left to right, John Gardiner, John Hodder, Alan Bowditch, John Tovey, Ken Gibson, Maureen Smith, Jacqueline James, Veronica Lucas, Daphne Hemmings, Unknown, Unknown, Marion Smith and George Hardacre. Front row: Anita Smith, Christine Lloyd, Tessa Wilcox, Jean Manning, Arvona Richardson, Pat Hiley, Marion Lovell, Ray Watts, Jean Richardson, Albert Clayton, Elaine Beckett, Lavinia Beach and Jeffrey Williams.

156. Celebrating the Centenary of Trinant Infants School 1892-1992. Back row, left to right, Edwina Heare, Joan Reynolds, Jenny Daniels, Tina Tutt, Barbara Richards, Sandra Wilkinson, Sarah Wilkinson, Lisa Taylor, Sandra Taylor, Rosalind Davies, Susan Dean, Elaine Rogers. Front row: Jackie Bryant, Gwyn Beddoes, Pauline Maguire, Nicola Holman, Christine Lewis, Pat Phillips (Headmistress), Lesley Pritchard, Elizabeth Davies, Jane Williams, Jenny Lewis and Ruth Elsey.

157. Trinant School St David's Day 1935. Teacher Miss Purnell, back row, left to right, Raymond Brown, Ted Morris, Lawrence Morrisey, Norman Gregory and Ira Williams. Second row: Charlie Rees, Lot Davies, Melvyn Shaw, Eileen Smith, Raymond Richards, Vera Price, Edwin Phillips, Thelda Rees, Horace Beach, Phillip Addis and John Beckett. Third row: Margaret Wilcox, Marion Perry, Thelma Morrisey, Grovenor Robinson, Mary Smith, Audrey Boucher, Cynthia Jenkins and Majorie Wiltshir. Front row: Pamela Rowley and Dora Tovey.

158. Trinant School St David's Day 1936. Back row, left to right, Clarence Beach, Gurnis Williams, Clive Holyfield, Clive Daniels, Elvet Morrisey, Brian Rowley, Garth Richard and Jean Davies. Middle row: Ralph Davies, John Gregory, John Smith, Cyril Morgan, Olive Morris, Brian Holyfield, Denzil Tovey and Penry Davies. Front row: Rhoda Harvey, Peggy Morrisey, Jeanette Phillips, Kate Morris, Faith Davies, Vera Jarrett, Marion Perry, Sylvia Weeks and Teacher Miss Purnell.

159. Trinant Infants School St David's Day 1985 with a display of Welsh national costume. Back row, left to right, Michael Hale, Darren Bond, Christopher Bates, Luke Gregory, Richard Lyons, Jay Madden and Geraint Morris. Second row: Kelly Davies, Sarah Lovell, Lorna Simmonds, Claire Griffiths, Rhiannon Rees, Louise Johnson, Joanne Dean, Emma Portman, Kerilee Lewis, Anne Marie Russell, Tammy Clayton, Julie Lovell. Third row: Emma Leader, Kerry Lawrence, Lisa Beddis, Tracey Tucker, Samantha Powell, Jodie Medcraft, Siân Lewis and Emma Gardner. Bottom row: Ross Hibbard, Leighton Stinchcombe, Gareth Snook, Michael Whitlock, Clive Tyler, Dean Rogers, Christian Morgan, Dean Brown, Jason Leadbeater and Simon DePlace.

160.   Trinant Junior School 1957. Back row, left to right, Barbara Watkins, Unknown, Jenny Lovell, Teacher Mrs C Mead. Middle row: Anthony Beach, Unknown, Paul Smith, Beverley Friend, Richard Hiley, Kevin Moyle, Unknown, Paul Robinson, David Morris and Maldwyn Rowlands. Front row: Gloria Tarling, Wendy Morris, Jean Ann Williams, Meryl Smith, Jean Williams, Gillian Lyons, Catherine James, Penelope Williams, Pat Rees, Moira Phelps, Sonja Mardy and Margaret Hale.

161.   Trinant Junior School Class 2 1958. Back row, left to right, Christopher Pritchard, David Smith, Teacher Miss Jenkins, Desmond Watkins and Paul Hale. Middle row: Angela Lloyd, Glenys Johns, Kerry Bates, Patricia Harvey, Christine Harvey, Linda Tudgay, Margaret Dowden, Delene Beach, Beryl Morgan, Bernice Poletti, Thelma Davies, Ann Friend and Ann John. Front row: Francis Jones, Martin Smitt, Bernard Morgan, David Hodder, Paul Watkins, Robert Lovell, Royston James, Terry Ackerman, Gerald Tarlin, Desmond Beddis and Paul Lyons.

162. Trinant Junior School Class 4 1957. Back, Headmaster Mr Taylor and Teacher Mr Jones. Back row, left to right, Rodney Payne, Leonard Brammer, Adrian Pritchard, Graham Clayton, Darryl James, Keith Davies, Glyn Rees, Dennis Friend, Graham Pullin, Lyndon Lloyd, Gilbert Moyle and Gary Lloyd. Front row: Tessa Wilcox, Geraldine Dowden, Lynda Smith, Sandra Payne, Sylvia Beach, Pat Clayton, Maureen Pritchard, Carol Williams, Ruth Hiley, Caroline Harwood, June Davies and Cora Jeremiah.

163. Trinant Junior School Class 4 1966. Back row, left to right, Mr Jones Teacher, David Morgan, Kerry Thomas, Martin Snook, Steven Matthews, Stanley Booth, Tudor Rees, John Filer, George Rees, Terry Collins, Paul Gregory and Mr Eric Finney Headmaster. Second row: Diane Brown, Deidre Bevan, Jacqueline Perkins, Sheila Evans, Gillian Filer, Gillian Hibble, Elaine Morris, Carol Ware, Virginia Roseblade, Carol Chick, Kathleen Coombes and Jacqueline Jones. Third row: Rosie Lyons, Kathryn Neal, Sandra Hillman, Denise Jones, Paulette Regnard, Susan Harvey, Joy Price, Cheryl Jones, Elaine Jenkins and Halena Junto. Bottom row: Leslie Robinson, Stuart Way, Nigel Morgan, Paul Bevan, Stephen Daniels, Graham Phillips and David Jenkins.

164. Trinant Junior School Class 2 1967. Back row, left to right, Simon Walters, Dean Thomas, Richard Owen, Darryl Waters, Shirley Harris, Trudy Goodwin, Julie Day and Michael Bates. Middle row: Francis Simmonds, Marjorie Haynes, Gail Gregory, Paula Mitchell, Mandy Woodford, Linda Reed, Ann Williams, Julie Smith, Christina Ellis and Teacher Mrs Davies. Bottom row: Paul Cartwright, Steven Porter, Andrew Randall, Dawn Lee, Carol Morgan, Kim Jones, Jane Hale and Jayne Cartwright.

165. Trinant Junior School 1968. Back row, left to right, Denise Rogers, Rhiannon Davies, Siân Potter, Julie Jones, Debra Woodford, Pat Beddis, Tracey John, Susan Davies and Suzanne Thomas. Second row: Derek Jones, Kevin Barnes, Tony Price, Timothy Warwick, Caroline Evans, Sharon Hockey, Michael Webb, Shirley Welsh, Jeremy Hockey and Teacher Mrs Langley. Third row: Sharon Lovell, Susan Madden, Valerie Chard, Natalie Way, Jennifer Parsons, Kim Hodder, Helen Lewis, Debbie Badham and Mandy Bowditch. Front row: Ray John, Weyrock Challenger, Carl Jeremiah, Grant Davies, Kim Weedon, Alan Woodhouse and Michael Erasmus.

166. Trinant Junior School 1969. Back row, left to right, Teacher Mrs Hall, Stuart Hughes, Alison James, Carl Cleverly, Martine Price, Mark James, Chris Welsh, Anthony Newman, Gareth Randell, Royston Harris, Martin Bolton the Teacher's name is unknown. Middle row: Debra Yates, Donna Lennon, Gail Williams, Steven Davies, Graham Parry, Lynda Davies, Clement Studholme, Michael Jenkins, Mark Whitlock, Andrew Jenkins and Sharon May. Front row: Jacqueline Weager, Lynette Ralph, Dena Mardy, Marilyn Williams, Melanie Baber, Lisa Roberts, Susan Booth, Kay Gregory, Maria Prosser and Kay Meacham.

167. Trinant Junior School Form 2 1987. Back row, left to right, Teacher Mr Barrowman, Mark Jones, Kevin Bates, Gareth Sheppard, Leigh Reynolds, Stephen Lane, Lee Jenkins, Richard Francombe, Michael Matthews and Headmaster Mr Lewis. Second row: Emma Portman, Clare Griffiths, Sheila McCullock, Joanne Dean, Louise Johnson, Jolene Pidgeon, Angela Beddis and Melanie Jones. Third row: Lorna Simmonds, Donna Watkins, Tracey Tucker, Bonny Daniel, Samantha Mathuen, Sarah Lovell, Sarah Hodder and Natalia Watkins. Front row: Michael Whitlock, Christian Morgan, Wayne Reynolds, Gareth Snook, Clive Tyler, Danny Williams and Michael Morgan.

168. Trinant Infants School Class 2 1989. Back row, left to right, Clinton John, Christopher Morgan, Jonathon Lawrence, James Chandler, David Taylor, Christopher Wake and Teacher Mrs Jardine. Middle row: Headmistress Mrs Bryant, Gareth Williams, Ian Matthews, Christian Sharpe, Carl Foxwell, Matthew Thomas, Darren Smith, Andrew Bearcroft. Front row: Natalie Beddis, Christine Jones, Jodie Clayton, Jenny Leader, Kate Elsey, Ruth Robinson, Kelly Sharp and Emma Tutt.

169. Trinant Infants School Nursery Class 1992. Back row, left to right, Teachers Mrs Price and Mrs Williams with pupils James Mogford, Natasha Leader, Charlotte Jones, Scott Evans, Michael Jones, Richard Parker, Kirsty Webley, Amy Taylor and Headmistress Mrs Phillips. Middle row: Emma Thomas, Rachael Sharp, Jonathon Woodhouse, Rees Morris, Greg Mitchell, James Leadbeater, Jason Jones and Lauren Webb. Front row: Sally Ann Pope, Danielle Shattock, Carla Dixon, Stephanie Thomas, Thomas Davies, Emma Maynard, Katie Davies, David Davies and Hannah Webb. Sitting on floor: Christopher Barnes, Kirsty Ralph and David Elsey.

CHAPTER 7

Aberbeeg and Llanhilleth

General View, Aberbeeg.

170. A most interesting general view of Aberbeeg as it appeared around 60 years ago. The buildings in the centre was the stable belonging to Webbs Brewery and to the right is the once impressive Hanbury Hotel. Some other premises in view and to be remembered are Kibby's, Jones the barber and Manchester House, the drapers shop.

19 Arches & River Aberbeeg

171. Another view from the 1920s we see the road from Aberbeeg to Llanhilleth supported by the 19 arches with the river Ebbw flowing below.

Memorial to Aberbeeg

They have torn out the heart of my
birthplace
In their quest to serve modern day man;
They have crippled it, kicked it, ruptured
and ripped it,
Spare a thought as you pass, if you can.

My school has quite gone, but it's memories
live on;
And perhaps one stands out very clear;
Of the head who burped his way through
the school
From a regular supply of Con's beer.

What have they done to Brondeg and the
Firs,
Places we loved with the passing of years;
As we passed from our street to Cwm-beeg
dingle brook,
They would always demand at least one
fond look.

Those banana-field days will be with us for
ever,
Where we savoured our rugby no matter
what weather;
Names like Shem and Jack Slocombe, in
our memory find birth,
As we recall their feats on this once
hallowed turf.

Now the goal-posts are down, and we're
kicked out of town;
They have built a nice hall and a club on
the ground;
A highway runs through, with a flyover
view
Of the features they've left, which believe
me, are few.

Christ Church can be seen on the way to
Pentwyn,
Trying it's best not to end up a ruin;
And behind it, our hospital peaceful and
calm,
Holds a welcome for all who require
healing balm.

And then ere you leave us, take one look if
you will,
At our dear Prims Chapel, there on the hill;
Clinging to the breast of Arael,
Testifying to the care and affection still
bestowed it,
By those who worship there.

It was here I heard the singing in those days
of want and strife,
That have been an inspiration as I've
journeyed through my life;
When I pay my scanty visit and I'm seated
in my pew,
I still can hear the voices of you, and you,
and you.

As you sang, Christ shall lead us in the days
of youth,
As you sang, Christ shall lead us in the paths
of truth,
As you sang, Christ shall lead us in the hour
of strife,
Upward to the light.

We've two friends here to stay though they
leave us every day,
And gurgle on their journey to the sea;
They depart here at the junction, having
served their function,
To baptise this place; God designed for me.

Ebbw Fach and Ebbw Vawr embrace each
other now
In seeming contentment and glee,
To remind me of the joy, and the scoldings
as a boy,
For playing in their muck at Aberbeeg.

172. The above is the work of well known local elocutionist Trevor Wilde and is reproduced with his kind permission.

Royal Oak Terrace and Trinant Hall, Llanhilleth

173. Royal Oak Terrace with its surrounding railway lines pictured in about 1910 with Trinant Hall, the Hewell family home in the background.

Llanhilleth & Aberbeeg New Parish Church

174. A view which shows the impressive stone-built Llanhilleth and Aberbeeg Parish Church. This late 14th century style building was erected in 1910 and by an order in Council in 1911, was substituted for that of nearby St. Illtyd's as the new Parish Church. To be noted in the picture is the absence of Aberbeeg Hospital which was yet to be built. The building at the bottom of the photograph is Pantddu Farm.

97

175. This is a panoramic view of Aberbeeg which has changed somewhat compared with the photograph on page 95. Above, it is about 1985 and the new road is under construction.

176. Many readers will of course remember the Hanbury Hotel and the adjacent Webbs Brewery. The brewery was in production from 1838 until closure in the early 1970s. The Hotel was demolished in 1990 and the area, once occupied by the brewery buildings is now the site of Aberbeeg's Medical Centre.

177. The popular and well used park at Llanhilleth. In the background are High Street and Maesycnew Terrace and the picture dates from the 1950s as evidenced by the railway lines which were still fully in use.

178. A Carnival at Llanhilleth circa. 1952. Back row, left to right, Hector Williams, (Clerk to Abertillery Council), Councillor Florence Brown, Mrs M Stephenson, Mrs M Edwards, Mrs G Edwards, Mrs M Beard, Mrs V Williams and Mrs F Prothero. Middle row: Denise Jones, Gwyneth Jones, Jill Morgan (Carnival Queen), Maureen Keeling, Joy Davies, Pauline Brown, Moira Morris, Beryl Minchin and David Hagland. Front row: Kay Donald, Gerald Edwards, George Challenger, Edward Brittain and Carol Thomas.

179. Aberbeeg Ambulance Station 1957. Left to right, Laurie Groves, Godfrey Fry, Cliff Saunders and Don Watts. The ambulance station was based at that time in the hospital grounds at Aberbeeg.

180. Domestic staff at the retirement of Matron G Body from Aberbeeg Hospital in the late 1950s. Back row, left to right, Dorothy Jones, Dilys Smith, Maureen Broome, Margaret Wiltshir, Jenny Daniels, Cissey Hughes, Heather Case, Rachael Williams and Kate Addis. Front row: Dulcie King, Violet Harvey, Harriet Watkins, Sarah Jones, Elizabeth Ellis, Matron Body, Joan Thomas, Edith Lewis, Phyllis Parry, Lily Baker, Winnie Lovell and Phyllis Noble.

181. Some partygoers at a Christmas function held at Aberbeeg Hospital in the early 1950s. This hospital was opened in 1922 and funded by the wholesome generosity of the local community. The hospital is still in use today, primarily in caring for the aged and infirm.

182. This is the Hanbury Hotel Darts Team displaying an array of trophies. Left to right are, back row, Eric Roberts, Denzil Tovey, David Davies, Philip Weybourne, Cliff Edwards, Jack Bayliss, Tom Welch and Howard Collins. Front row: Mrs Collins, Ken Hiley, Adolphus Carpenter, Bert Hiley and Lyndon Robinson.

183./184. Two photographs of business premises belonging to local entrepreneurs, the Kibby family. In the photograph on the left is their first grocers and bakers shop which was situated near the railway bridge in Aberbeeg and outside are Harry and Louise Kibby with their sons Arthur and John in about 1930. On the right is the small filling station also part of the original business which was one day to become a small empire. Son Arthur's policy after the war and with the gradual end to food rationing was 'pile it high and sell it cheap!' Thus the first examples of supermarket style shopping appeared in the valleys.

185. Within 10 years Kibby's was a renowned chain grocer with shops in Abertillery (as seen above), Ebbw Vale, Brynmawr, Pontypool, Cwmbran, Newport and beyond, with the three brothers Arthur, Harry and John ever driving the company forward. These supermarkets rose to a total of 15 and soon caught the eye of a national chain, Jones and Porter, part of Unigate Ltd. A merger took place and so led to a total of eighty supermarkets throughout the country with Arthur Kibby as managing director. The photograph above shows the former shop in Somerset Street Abertillery and some of the assistants to be seen are: Meryl Hayward, Cynthia Micheli (hiding behind the scales), and Ann Jones.

186.   One of the earliest known photographs of the Kibby grocery business is this of the horsedrawn bread delivery cart pictured at Pentwyn Road, Trinant in about 1900. Little did these two employees know the extent to which their meagre mode of transport at Trinant would eventually reach.

187.   A few years later and the company transport is motorised. The Kibby empire continued to expand relentlessly even reaching Scotland and was to see further amalgamation, this time with Gardners of Bristol and Arthur becoming head of a company of some 400 stores with brother Harry becoming Area Director, South East. Davies Printers Ltd., (owners of the publishing company of this book) and another local family business well remember the positive working relationships with the Kibby organisation and its rise to stardom in the supermarket world and its lifetime policy of 'caring for the customer'. Arthur Kibby eventually retired to Bournemouth and died there in 1993.

188. Unfortunately the author has been unable to trace the names of the participants on this occasion but here are the crowds at Glandwr Street celebrating the end of the war in Europe in May 1945. Despite food rationing the residents have triumphed in providing well for this historic event.

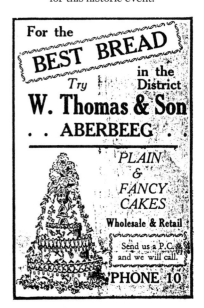

189. The Brynhyfryd Secondary Modern School Football Team 1968 and the players are left to right, back row, Martin Hewins, Chris Randall, Gareth Phillips, Steve Richards, Mike Powell, Alan Curtis and Mervyn Leadbeater. Front row: Steve Haines, Gareth Francombe, Aneurin Jenkins, Leslie Britton, Paul Martin and Peter Francombe.

190.   Commercial Road Llanhilleth from the year 1905 when there was no motor traffic hurtling up and down the street and it was safe for children to pose for the photographer.

191.   One of the oldest churches in Wales is that of St Illtyd's near Brynithel, where worship is said to have taken place since the 5th century. This was the ancient and original parish church of Aberbeeg and Llanhilleth with registers going back to the year 1733. Built of stone in the Gothic style, it has seen many restorations throughout its long history, particularly in quite recent times.

192. This is one of the first buses owned by The Griffin Bus Company of Brynmawr, with its solid tyres en-route for Llanhilleth in the 1920s. For the enthusiast, this particular Dennis bus started life as a military truck and was used during the first world war. It was later converted to a 32 seat passenger vehicle to be purchased by Griffin in 1922 and remained in service until 1928.

193. A Jones's Bus makes its way up the hill to Trinant with Aberbeeg in the background. Locals will recall the tragedy that befell the family-owned bus company in 1950 when three of the four sons of the founder of the company, Webb Jones, were killed in the Llandow air disaster.

CHAPTER 8

Crumlin

194. Crumlin Square and the Low Level Crossing, as the scene looked at the end of the last century. On the left of the picture can be seen an old farmhouse which is now the site of the present day Workman's Institute.

195. This is another look at the Square, a few years later than the photograph on the previous page. Below is an advertisement for the Crumlin Viaduct Works dating from the year 1876.

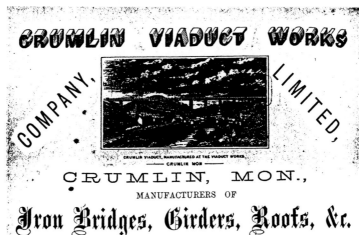

CRUMLIN VIADUCT WORKS

COMPANY, LIMITED,

CRUMLIN VIADUCT, MANUFACTURED AT THE VIADUCT WORKS, CRUMLIN MON

CRUMLIN, MON.,

MANUFACTURERS OF

Iron Bridges, Girders, Roofs, &c.

The following is a List of some of the Principal Bridges Manufactured at these Works.

No. of Bridges.	Bridges for whom and where sent.	No. of Spans.	Width of Spans.	Tons Weight.
1	Crumlin Viaduct as above, Great Western Railway .	10	150	—
1	Blackfriars, London, L. C. & D. Railway . . .	5	202	2704
120	Government in Buenos Ayres	Various.		6900
69	Rome & Ancona Railway	,,		2713
1	Sent to India (Barrakur)	9	155	—
1	East Indian Railway	14	89	623
1	Pernambuco	17	60	364
1	Bombay & Baroda Railway	10	60	227
1	Kidderpore & Ballinghatta	2	132	180
1	Lelajun in India	10	56	254
1	New Ross, Ireland	5	100	1000
1	Murray River, Australia	5	121	555
1	Wolkoff, Great Russian Railway	5	165	1500

196. Crumlin High Level Station photographed in 1960, with a passenger train at the platform during its journey from Neath to Pontypool. By this time, for safety reasons, traffic over the viaduct had been restricted to a speed of 8 mph and the original double track reduced to one.

197. The Low Level Station in about 1954 with a 57xx Class panier locomotive hauling the coaches. The valley lines from Ebbw Vale and Brynmawr merged at Aberbeeg and the tracks then continued down the valley through Crumlin Low Level and all stations to Newport.

198./199. A 1950s view of The Square, Crumlin and its famous viaduct. Ideas for a railway bridge to cross the valley were first mooted by the Newport, Abergavenny and Hereford Railway Co., in 1850, in order to gain access to the rich coal deposits of Glamorgan. Noted design engineers T W Kennard, a Mr Clayton and Mr Liddell were recruited for the task. Work commenced with initial financial backing of £40,000 and the first pier was fixed in December 1853. This was to be known as the 'Isabella Pier' so named after Lady Isabella Fitzmaurice who officially opened it.

200./201. To illustrate just some of the improvements and changes that have taken place during this century, here are two views of Crown Street Crumlin. Above, is the craggy road surface, houses with no TV aerials and the prestigious viaduct of the year 1900 whilst pictured below is a view from the same spot in 1995.

202./203. Two 'Bird's Eye' views of Crumlin with some interesting comparisons to be made. Above, we can see that the houses at Treowen have yet to be built and Pritchards Brewery still stands. In the lower photograph readers will see the Miners Institute in the centre and the old Palace Picture House bottom left. Films, stage shows and boxing tournaments were some of the one-time attractions held here but unfortunately, with changing tastes in leisure and entertainments, the venue fell into decline and was to become known locally as the 'White Elephant'.

Crumlin from High Level.

204./205. The completed viaduct was opened for traffic on June 1st 1857, a Whit Monday and it is recorded as being an event of immense celebration and rejoicing with some 20,000 spectators attending and watching the open-top carriages being pulled along. Cannon fire was heard to thunder across the valley the whole day. The final cost of this construction was £62,000 which measured some 200 feet high and 1650 feet long. Much of the material used, hailed from Blaenavon Ironworks, world famous for its quality products. This feat of engineering was to last more than 100 years until the era of railway rationalisation and the last train crossed in June 1964.

206./207. Some later observations overlooking Crumlin, taken from the site of the railway viaduct. Above, demolition of the Palace Picture House is well advanced but the low level station and the railway lines to Newport are still intact. Below, is the scene in 1995 and even this is changing rapidly as major roadworks are currently in progress putting yet another face on the district.

208. The former Wesleyan Chapel, Hillside. The first chapel was a wooden construction followed by the 'Iron Church' and then, to meet ever growing congregations, the stone-built church above, was opened in 1900. Like so many places of worship, it is now closed and has been converted to a private residence.

209. Noddfa English Baptist Church Crumlin 1918. On the far right is Albert Jones of Kendon, and the Pastor in the centre is the Reverend J W T Treharne. In recent years the building has finally been converted to the Crumlin Rugby Club.

210. Crumlin High Level Primary School Class P5 1994. Back row, left to right: Aimee Thomas, Owen Hooper, Craig Roscoe, Ian Thomas, Christopher Davies, Hannah Lewis and Annika Davies. Third row: Teacher Mrs Lampard, Gregg James, Greg Thomas, Michelle Frost, David Irwin, Michael Frost, Andrew Edwards, Kayley Beach, Darren Jones and Mr Tilley the Headmaster. Second row: Gareth Davies, Ryan Gajda, Richard Clayton, Christopher Duke, Sherry Davies, Christopher Evans, Rhys Powell, Carly Plant and Darren Griffiths. Front row: Hywel Curtis, Laura George, Scott Goodwin, Rachael Meredith, Rachael Jones, Craig Buckley, Gemma Keeling and Darren Farmer.

211. Crumlin High Level School Football Team 1919. The teacher in the centre with the trilby hat is Sam Skuse of Trinant.

212. Kendon Junior Rugby Team 1929-30. Back row, left to right: Mr Wilson, John Ford, Harry Harris. Second row: Darkie Bernard, Tom Phelps, Bryn Lane, Billy Henry Lewis, Stan White, Reg Higgins, Charlie Jenkins, John Nash, Mr Porter, Cyril Jones, Alf Nash, Tom Duckham (Senior) and Cy Phelps. Third row: Jack Phelps, Bill Ford, Percy Kenvin, Dai Price, Don Phelps and Jack Porter. Front row: Howard Nash and Tom Duckham.

213. This photograph was taken at the Kendon around 1918. Regretfully little is known of its origin but perhaps a reader or two will recognise a parent or grandparent?

214. Kendon Carnival 1950. Back row, left to right: D Jones, J Fricker, R Jones, Unknown, F Adams, Mrs B Jones and Mrs D Lewis. Middle row: J Jones, I Lewis, W Lewis, Mrs Smith and T Challenger. Front row: Unknown, S Smith, Mrs Ackerman, Mrs E Price and Mrs Edwards.

215. This is a photograph of Charles Jones and his family at Croespenmaen Farm in 1910. Unfortunately the farm was completely destroyed by fire in 1947 when it was owned by Mr Fred Thomas.

216. A rural scene taken at the village of Manmoel in 1948 when the sheep population appears to out number that of human beings!

217. Oakdale, once described in its youth as a 'Model Village', grew to be a thriving mining community through the 20th century, thanks to the extensive colliery that at one time provided some 2000 jobs, producing one million tons of coal in a year. The colliery commenced coal production in 1911 and went on to become one of South Wales' major suppliers of coking coal to the steel industry. The colliery finally closed in 1990 despite massive investments by the National Coal Board.

218. The scene above would be more recognisable today as the Texaco filling station. This particular photograph is from 1952 when the owner was Mr Val Williams and seen here at the old style 'Regent' pumps are Mr Williams' brother and sister George and Shirley.

219./220. The purpose built colliery village of Oakdale was originally built and designed by the Oakdale Navigation Colliery Ltd in the 1900s. The layout of the village with tree-lined streets and houses with decorative front gardens, were unique for a South Wales mining town at the time. Both of these photographs were taken during the 1920s do well to illustrate a certain amount of opulence at Oakdale for the period, despite the harsh economic times about to dawn on the community.

221.   This is a photograph of the original Oakdale Institute which started life as a library in a hut built near the colliery in 1912. Contributions of 1d (½p) per week were made by the working men of the district and the first major investment, that of a billiards table was made. The Institute was soon to become the centre of the village social life and there was much discussion about the need to expand, particulary for a fully stocked library to help educate one and all. In 1916, the Tredegar Iron and Coal Co. was approached for financial assistance and they eventually agreed to make a loan of £3000 towards the total cost of £6463 for the project. The new buildings, which housed a reading room, concert hall, 6 billiard tables and refreshments, was officially opened on 10th September 1917 by Mr R S Tallis, Managing Director of the Tredegar Co.

The Institute was a resounding success and even attracted a royal visitor in 1920, HRH Prince Albert, later to become King George VI. Strict rules were put in place by a strong and loyal committee, determined to preserve the good name of the establishment. There is however one act of early vandalism recorded at a 1921 dance, when a hand basin was wrenched from the wall. Called before the committee the accused stated 'I don't think it was me who did it'. Nevertheless, he was curtly informed that he had actually been found with the basin lying across his chest and no further defence was offered! In the early 1920s the film entertainment industry swept the country and the increasing population of Oakdale called for its own cinema. Severe economic conditions prevailed for a number of years and it was 1927 before the cinema was built adjacent to the existing building, with an orchestra being employed for the showing of the then silent films. There was even talk of constructing a swimming pool but the continued economic depression throughout the 1930s prevented any further expansion.

However social and economic life did recover, prosperity returned to the Institute and the final payment of all loans to the Tredegar Co., was made in 1945, a momentous occasion indeed. Post war economic wealth, particularly the highly successful Oakdale Colliery and its workers continued to make the Institute a 'going concern', with Music and Dramatic societies being formed.

However the mid 1950s saw the first signs of change in village life with a new and permanent period of decline. The library closed in 1967 and the cinema gave way to the new craze of bingo. The entire building was closed down after more than 60 years of service to the community and acquired by Islwyn Borough Council. Fortunately in 1989, although the cinema building could not be saved, the 1917 Institute construction was dismantled stone by stone and transported to the St Fagans Museum, Cardiff and 6 years of restoration work is near completion.

THE OAKDALE WORKMEN'S INSTITUTE.

The Committee of the above request the pleasure of
the Company of

Mr. S. Hill

at Oakdale on the occasion of the

Opening of the New Institute,

by F. L. DAVIES, Esq., (Director of the Tredegar
Iron and Coal Co., Ltd., on MONDAY, SEPT. 10th,
1917, at 4 p.m.   Lunch at 5 p.m.
                          A. McDONALD, Secretary,
6, Syr Dafydd Avenue, Oakdale.

222./223. Above is the Institute and Picture House as they looked in their prime at Oakdale in 1945. Below it is 50 years on and the original Institute building, nears reconstruction at its new site at the Museum of Welsh Life at St Fagans, Cardiff. After restoration to its former glory, the structure is soon to be opened to the public once again.

224. A rare occasion would be a Royal visit to Oakdale. Here HRH Prince Albert later to be crowned King George VI and father of our present Queen leaves the Institute after his visit in 1920.

225. It is likely that this photograph, taken outside the Institute was taken during the 1920s and the boys here may well have been among the army of the unemployed at the time. At the handlebars is Evan 'Yanto' Davies who was a shot-firer at Oakdale Colliery. The design of the motorcycle shows what rapid progress has been made in that field of transport!

226./227. During the year of publication of this book, there were street parades abound to celebrate the 50th anniversary of VE Day. Both of these photographs were taken at some original parties held at Oakdale to mark the end of the war in 1945. Above, the children are pictured at Maesygarn whilst below that same event is being observed at Rhiw-syr-Daffyd Avenue.

228. Members of the Oakdale British Legion outside their headquarters. It was known as the Bomb and Dagger and this photograph was taken during the early 1930s. It is now the site of Ye Olde Forge Inn and Motel.

229. Oakdale RFC 1920-21. Back row, left to right: Unknown, Nobby Hall, Unknown, Unknown, Richard Lucas, Walter Sims, Bob Parry, Unknown and Dai Richards. Second row: Trainer Tom Morgan, Alf Rogers, Roger Sims, Roger Taylor, Jack Lewis (DCM), George Williams, Unknown, Unknown, Reg Yorath, Jack Stocks and Unknown. Third row: Dan Jones, Tom (Jonah) Jones, Bill Griffiths, Bert Love (Captain), Obby Sims, Unknown and Bryn Watkins. Front row: Unknown, Unknown, Charlie Noakes and Bill Sleeman. The author apologises for being unable to identify a few of the players but would welcome any information regarding their names and he may be contacted through the publishers of this book.

230. Rhiw-syr-Dafydd School First Football Team 1919/20. Standing, left to right: Jack Smith with Mr Dan Jones (Schoolteacher), Trevor (Hocka) Thomas, George Phillips, George Pontin, Mr Evans (School Teacher) and Dai Moore. Front row: Wilfred Green, George Morgan, Ivor Tudball, Mars Smith, Robert Painter and Ivor Yorath.

231. Oakdale RFC 1954. Back row, left to right: Graham Parry, Harry Davies, Lyndon Howls, John Beckett, Ralph Badham and Jim Smith. Second row: Ken Barnfield, Dennis Kenvin, Gary Poulton, Haydn Morgan and Lionel Beckett. Front row: Howell Jenkins, Eddie Ralph, Glyn Morgan and Gwyn Jones.

232. Mr Austin Perrott third from left exhibiting on open day at Usk College Show. He was a bee expert and started keeping bees at the age of fifteen and continued with his pastime until he died in 1978 aged sixty-eight.

233. The Co-op Shop at Oakdale ceased trading on the 20 May 1995. Mrs Cynthia Willmot and Mary Mitchell close the doors for the last time.

Acknowledgements

Many people have helped in the production of this book through their willingness to provide time, information and personal photographs. Grateful thanks are extended to the undermentioned and sincere apologies are offered to anyone who may have been inadvertently omitted.

The author would very much welcome the loan of any further photographs etc. from readers who might wish to see them published in a further volume of this book. He may be contacted at the address of the publishers.

R. Ball, Mrs L Beach, Mr J Clayton, Mrs G Cook, Mrs S Cook, Mrs A Davies, Mrs D Davies, Mrs Dolly Davies, Mr E Davies, Mr L Davies, Mr R Davies, Mrs V Davies, Mrs E Erasmus, Mrs A Fry, Mrs B Friend, Mrs L Gardner, Mrs R Garland, Mr G Hallett, Mrs M Harris, Mrs P Harwood, Mrs C Hatton, Mr J Holyfield, Mrs M Holyfield, Mrs B Jenkins, Mrs C Jones, Mr D Jones, Mrs P Jones, Mr R Jones, Mr H Kibby, Mrs M Kibby, Mrs D Leadbeater, Mrs C Lewis, Mrs P Lewis, Mrs V Lewis, Mrs V Matthews, Mr W Mayberry, Mr D Moore, Mrs E Morgan, Mrs T Morgan, Mr E Morrisey, Mr G Nash, Mrs E Padfield, Mrs J Padfield, Mrs P Page, Mrs C Perrott, Mrs A Poletti, Mr W Price, Mr W Pritchard, Mrs J Porter, Mrs W Rees, Mrs B Richards, Mrs D Robinson, Mrs E Rogers, Mr M Rowlands, Mrs J Smith, Mr R Smith, Mr C Taylor, Mr R Taylor, Mrs O Thatcher, Mr J Toomer, Mrs T Tutt, Trinant Sports Social Club, Mrs E Watts, Mrs B Weybourne, Mr T Wilde, Mrs P Williams, Mr G Williams, Miss S Williams and Mr S Williams.